Dear Mateo,

Sending you lots of sunshine and fairy magic! :)

Suzanne Alexander Heaton
2010

The ABC Field Guide to Faeries

to

Inspiring reminders of respect for ourselves, each other and the environment.

By Susanne Alexander-Heaton

Artwork by Chantal T. Gabriell

Acknowledgements

A special thank you to the Shell Foundation who have helped make the printing of this edition possible • www.shellfoundation.org

A note from the author, Susanne Alexander-Heaton • www.abcfaeries.com

I am so incredibly grateful to Sarah who helped to inspire the writing of this book as well as to Sarah's parents who allowed me to dedicate this book in her memory, to Chantal whose illustrative magic helped the faeries come to life on the page, to my good friend Verena for being my ultimate confidant and earth angel, to my husband for standing by me through the entire process, to my mother for instilling the love of reading, art, and creativity and to my late father for his visionary leadership, especially in soil and water conservation. Although both Sarah and my father have passed on, I feel their presence all around me and I am truly humbled by their never-ending support on this journey.

A note from the designer, Chantal T. Gabriell • www.seashinedesign.com

There's never a dull moment when working with faeries, pixies and gremlins! Thank you, inspiring wee folk, Gaby, Phoenix and Lily Blue.

While never having met Sarah, I have seen how brightly she lives on in the hearts of others as a beautiful reminder of the enduring nature of love.

Art & Design by Chantal T. Gabriell, SeaShine Design, www.seashinedesign.com

Photo credits: please refer to back page

Manufactured by Friesens Corporation in Altona, Canada
September, 2009
Job # 47953

ISBN 978-0-9813048-0-9
1. Education/General

In Loving Memory of

Sarah Lisa Foidart

1991 – 2003

Sarah was a 12-year-old girl from a rural Manitoba community. She courageously fought a battle against a very rare brain tumour but, unfortunately, she did not win. Sarah touched many people in her very short life. She was known for her mischievous playfulness and from a young age was a real trooper when it came to taking hikes; she so loved being in nature.

Sarah had, and continues to have a deep impact on my life. The night after she passed away she came to me in a dream, totally free from pain and back to her giggly old self. In the dream, she was twirling around in a meadow of wildflowers and said to me: "Susanne, I have faery wings instead of angel wings because faery wings are so much easier to run and play around in!"

That dream is as vivid to me today as it was the night I had it. After I had it, I started to research everything I could about faeries. One of the things I discovered was that they are considered "nature's angels". And it was while out on a nature excursion that the inspiration for writing *The A, B, C Field Guide to Faeries* came to me. I could not write the ideas down fast enough! I knew that Sarah was helping me tap into this creative channel.

This book is lovingly dedicated to that courageous young lady, who will forever live on in my heart, and who encompasses the character traits of each and every one of the faeries you will see and read about in the following pages. It is my hope that Sarah will touch every reader's heart with her magic and inspire and motivate you to treat yourself, each other and the environment with respect.

Long may Sarah's spirit live on.

In love, light and enlightenment,

Susanne

A is for two faery sisters, Avriel and Ataija
[Av'ree'el] ◆ [Ah'tay'jah]

Avriel and Ataija teach the importance of balance,
By showing off their own unique weather talents.
Avriel creates lightning which many people fear,
While Ataija causes thunder when Avriel is near.

Avriel and Ataija's warning message:

"Mother Nature is a very mighty thing,
So treat her like you would a great king!
Her power with weather needs to be respected,
As she can do many things that can be unexpected."

B is for Buzzalina ◆ [Buzz'a'lean'ah]

Buzzalina is called Buzzy by all of her friends,
As she loves to have fun and easily blends.
Between practical jokes and dozens of smiles,
Buzzy's laughter rings out for miles and miles.

Buzzy firmly believes:

*"Whether it be in the sun, the rain, or the snow,
You should always have fun, wherever you go.
Think of all the amusing things you can do,
To bring much laughter and happiness too."*

C is for Camilio ◆ [Ka'meal'ee'oh]

Camilio, who is known for his playful laughter,
Can be found on the river as an avid rafter!
After each mini waterfall, rapid or drop,
You hear his "Woo-Hoo" above the treetops.

Camilio's mantra:

*"Take time each day to play and to laugh,
If you're lucky like me, you may be in a raft!
Please follow your heart as you go on your way,
Then you will find pleasure in every day."*

D is for Desiderada ◆ [Dez'ee'dah'rata]

Desiderada is one, who loves to dance,
To some she may seem to be in a trance.
She twirls around in a soft summer breeze,
And buzzes about like the bumble bees.

Desiderada knows:

"We are all only dancing on this earth a short time,
So be sure to dance with a happy song in your mind.
Dance loudly, dance strongly to the heavens above,
But most of all, dance with your heart full of love."

E is for Echinops ◆ [Ek'e'nops]

Echinops is a very inquisitive little faery,
Who is very excited about his latest discovery.
Each butterfly he finds likes different flowers,
Due to their preference for nectar and colours.

Echinops says:

"Build a butterfly garden with a mixture of plantings,
To attract these insects which are so enchanting.
Monarch butterflies prefer to feed on milkweed,
So plant some of this and you'll fulfill all their needs."

F is for Faleryana ◆ [Fall'air'ee'anna]

Faleryana can be seen in the time we call fall,
Of all the colours, red is her favorite one of all.
She loves to shout her colours out, so strong and loud,
Especially on the Maple leaf of which she is so proud.

Faleryana whispers:

*"Please be not afraid when the leaves drop from the trees,
As the leaf finished its purpose but its spirit never leaves.
With each spring and summer, the leaf's memory is renewed,
And my magic starts again, as the leaf becomes earth's food."*

G is for Gabriella ◆ [Gay'brie'el'ah]

Gabriella is fond of animals like horses, dogs and cats.
Her tender glances feel to them like many loving pats.
When you see your pet is gazing into a vacant land,
You can bet your bottom dollar Gabriella is close at hand.

Gabriella coos:

"When you pet any animal there can be,
You will also be connecting directly with me.
If you are kind to animals for all your living days,
I will reward you, in many loving ways."

H is for Hillaria ◆ [Hill'air'ee'ah]

Hillaria is the happiest faery you will ever meet,
As she laughs so much she barely has time to eat!
It shocked her that when some humans grow old,
Their laughter decreases over a full ten-fold.

Hillaria lovingly says:

"Don't lose the ability to laugh and to play,
Learn to laugh like me more than ten times a day.
Have you taken the time to laugh at all today?
If not, please do and you'll feel better right away!"

I is for Ioneia ◆ [Eye'oh'knee'ah]

Ioneia, who is a faery courageous and bold,
Seeks comfort in a lion's mane when she's cold.
She is respected and thought of as very majestic,
As she puts herself first, when things get too hectic.

Ioneia's advice:

"Make sure to take some time every day,
That is just for you to keep stress far away.
If you don't take really good care of yourself,
Your plans to help others will stay on the shelf."

J is for Joylene ◆ [Joy'lean]

Joylene is a faery found in the joy of a child,
As her temperament is so innocent and mild.
When a baby expresses its first pure hearted laugh,
A new faery is born to help with her tasks!

Joylene pleads:

"To all children, please be their pure sense of joy,
As this cannot be obtained from a shiny new toy.
Instead it is something that must come from the heart,
Like spending time with the child and doing your part."

K is for Kiara ◆ [Key'air'ah]

Kiara, who is a creative and intuitive faery,
Can tell instantly when someone is too wary.
Kiara immediately knows just what she needs to do,
As she paints beautiful scenes to say she loves you.

Kiara says:

"When rain comes along and makes you feel sad,
Don't worry, as soon, I will help to make you glad.
I get to paint the majestic rainbows way up above,
After there's been rain, to show that you are loved."

L is for Lanternia ◆ [Lan'ter'knee'ah]

Lanternia, who comes out only at night,
Illuminates like a glowing flashlight.
She uses fireflies and click beetles too,
So she's popular at functions the faeries go to.

Lanternia says:

"Whether it be a flashlight, a beetle, or a firefly,
All can help to light up the dark evening sky.
Each of us has our own luminous light,
To help us shine through the darkest of nights."

M is for Michael ◆ [Mike'el]

Michael, who enjoys sports and is happiest outside,
Loves to play all day on the skateboard he rides.
He picks up the litter he finds along the pathways,
As he wants earth to be clean for all of its days.

Michael's message:

"Do whatever you can to make the world a cleaner place,
Get caught up in this challenge, as if it were a race.
Pick up any garbage that you happen to see,
And all will be blessed by what comes to be."

N is for Namastasia ◆ [Naw'ma'stay'jah]

Namastasia, who is as powerful by day as she is by night,
Wants you to know everything will always be all right.
She wants you to love yourself fully inside and out,
And do it each day without the slightest of doubt.

Namastasia wants you to repeat:

*"I honour the guru that's deep in my heart,
As I'm like a priceless, masterpiece of art.
I'm only human, so I will make mistakes,
But I'll practice forgiveness with all that it takes."*

O is for Orchestrata ◆ [Or'ka'stra'ta]

Orchestrata, who helps all of nature make a great symphony,
Is always practicing what his next composition will be.
If you open your heart, and quiet your mind,
You will hear music that has stood the test of time.

Orchestrata hums:

"Listen close to my music and soon you will hear,
How Mother Nature holds each of us ever so near.
She calls to us in mysterious and playful ways,
As she wants us to respect her for all of our days."

P is for Passionella ◆ [Pash'on'el'ah]

Passionella is courageous and always on the run.
She loves to go on escapades having lots of fun.
Whether skydiving, rock climbing, hang gliding or such,
She is up to the challenge because she loves life so much.

Passionella's advice:

"This life of yours is no dress rehearsal,
So, quick, make haste and think universal.
Write down all the things that you want to do,
Then make a master plan to see them come true."

Q is for Quinella ◆ [Kwin'el'ah]

Quinella, who is the ruler of the oceans, rivers and seas,
Can often be heard whispering in the gentlest breeze.
He is kind and soft yet speaks of the great things,
That water provides for all living beings.

Quinella's plea:

"Don't dump in the water what you wouldn't drink,
It is time for all humans to wake up and think.
What is dumped in the water ends up inside you,
Honour this precious resource for what it can do."

R is for Randolph ◆ [Ran'doll'f]

Randolph is a faery who is linked to the raven,
With his magical powers he creates a safe haven.
Randolph can do what he sets his mind to,
And he asks that very same thing of you.

Randolph's counsel:

*"Whenever the night seems just a little too long,
Call out for me and my raven to sing our magical song.
You are a child of Great Spirit from the heavens above,
You must never, ever forget that you are dearly loved."*

S is for Susanne ◆ [Sue'zan]

Susanne the sunshine faery, often can be found,
In fields of sunflowers, down upon the ground.
Sunflowers follow the sun, through the course of the day,
So wherever the sun is in the sky, they point that way.

Susanne believes:

"We are all connected like beams of light to the sun,
So we must be kind to others for we're all truly one.
No matter where we come from in terms of colour or race,
We're linked one and all to this brilliant light place."

T is for Transparianthus ◆ [Trans'peary'an' thus]

Transparianthus, who can manifest all of our dreams,
Can be found floating around magnificent pine trees.
He wants all of your wildest dreams to come true,
So believe this in your heart and in all that you do.

Transparianthus says:

"If you have a special dream, then request it from me,
If it is for your highest good, it'll surely come to be.
While you wait patiently for your dream to come true,
Take positive action and see what happens to you."

U is for Uniqueuella ◆ [U'neek'you'el'ah]

Uniqueuella is a faery that is very rare to be found,
As he flies with the unicorns way above the ground.
Instead of seeing himself as different or strange,
He embraces who he is and refuses to change.

Uniqueuella's message:

*"If people tell you that you just don't belong,
Just say thanks, and go on singing your own song.
You are magical, beautiful, mystical and bright,
So shine out strongly with your unending light."*

V is for Verena ◆ [Va'ree'na]

Verena, who is connected to the heavens like a dove,
Sometimes can be seen in the stars up above.
Whether it be the Big Dipper or Orion's Belt,
Verena's nightly presence can always be felt.

Verena's message:

"If I send down to you a bright falling star,
Make a special wish as I'm listening from afar.
Believe in your heart that I will make it come true,
And the best of the best will be bestowed unto you."

W is for Willow ◆ [Will'oh]

Willow is lanky, lean and difficult to see,
As he plays hide and seek amongst willow trees.
He listens intently for sounds all around,
Hoping no garbage gets thrown on the ground.

Willow says:

"If you're walking along a great hiking trail,
Be kind to nature and let common sense prevail.
Throwing trash on the ground destroys my home,
So please don't do this on any trails that you roam."

 is for Xiemena ◆ [Ze'me'na]

Xiemena, the faery who helps when you are sick,
Overflows with compassion to help you up quick.
She has unconditional love, all you need to do is ask,
And she'll do her best to help, with all your healing tasks.

Xiemena whispers:

*"Simply believe there are powers here to cure,
To get you on your feet, of this you can be sure.
To thank me for the healing that I do for you,
Respect yourself, others and the environment too."*

Y is for Yolanda ◆ [Yo'land'ah]

Yolanda is the protector of our beautiful lands,
Like the mountains, the plains and the desert sands.
She is a peaceful warrior that needs to be revered,
So treat her with respect and you'll have nothing to fear.

Yolanda's plea:

"Be kind to the land that surrounds you all around,
Never throw your garbage over earth's sacred ground.
Mother Earth has many gifts available for you,
So respect her with everything it is that you do."

Z is for Zoryana ◆ [Zore'ee'anna]

Zoryana can be found amongst a great number of plants,
As she loves eating apples and watching leaf cutter ants!
She knows plants are necessary for a healthy environment,
As they provide oxygen for breathing requirements.

Zoryana's message:

*"Be wise and plant some flowers, bushes, or trees,
To make food and homes for animals, birds and bees.
Plants also help humans to be healthy and to grow,
May many plants surround you wherever you go."*